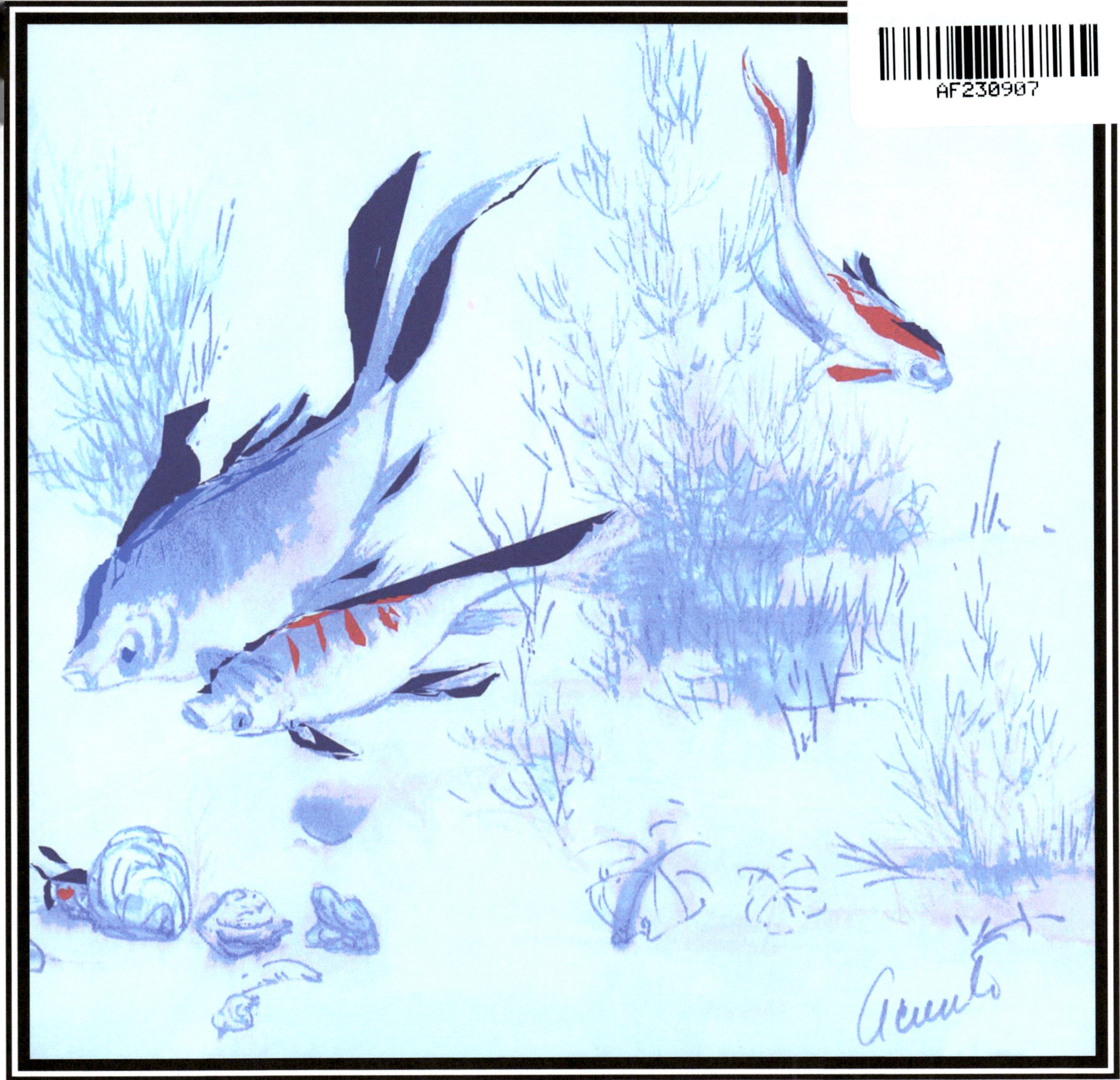

CHINA SONG

Life's Lessons with Original Pictures

Author/Artist
Ida Lillian Acunto

DEDICATION

To my dear teacher and friend Pei Liang who brought the world of eternal beauty into my life.

I leave these pages to my Family as a reminder that true Beauty really runs skin deep.

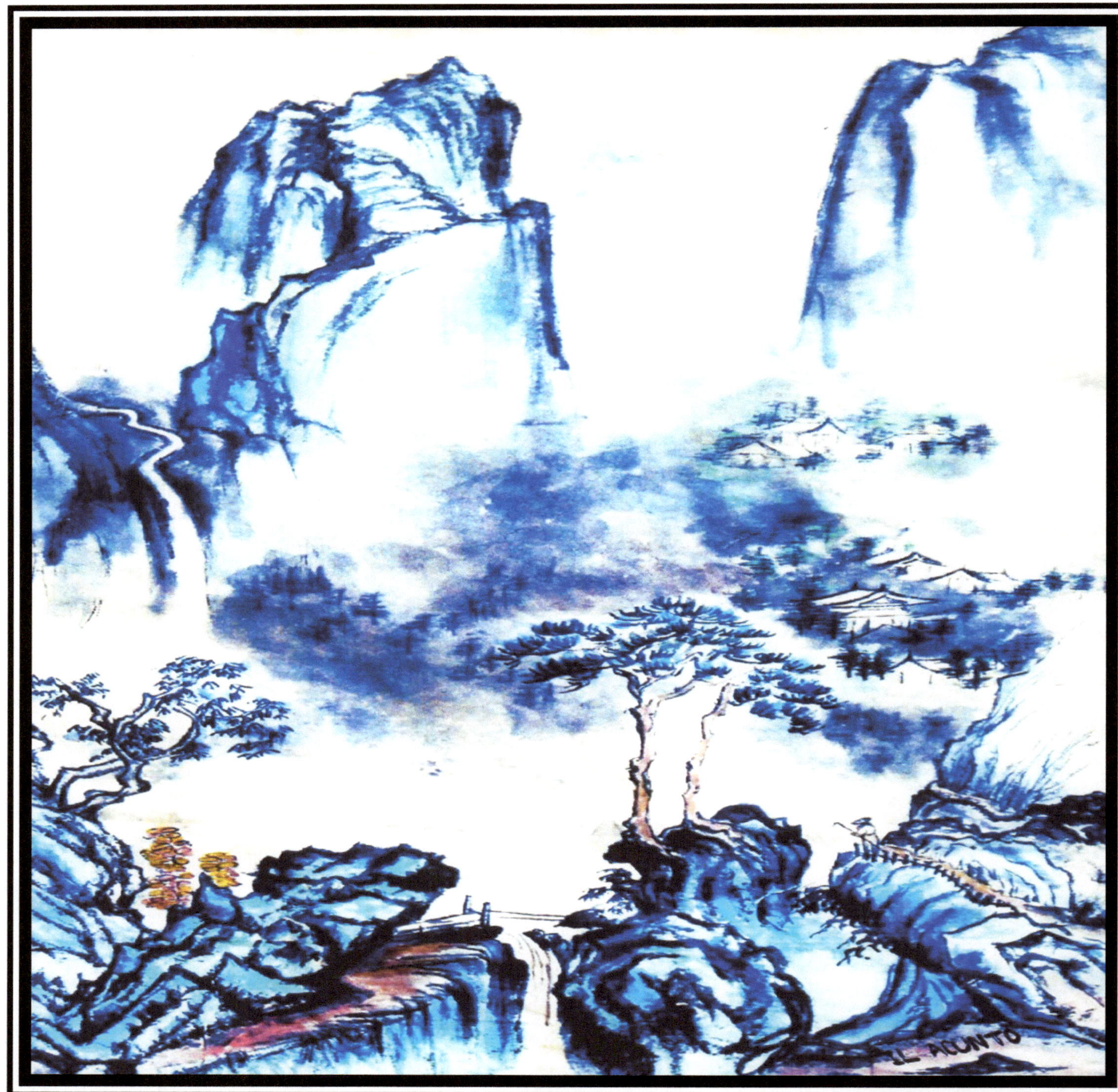

BLUE MOUNTAINS

In 1970, I was a single, divorced parent supporting myself and my two children first as a Teacher, Psychologist, and then Administrator of a secondary comprehensive high school in Long Island, New York. I loved my vocation almost as much as I loved art. The need to pursue my artistic interests while working brought me to New York University taking a class with the Chinese Master Teacher Pei Liang.

Pei Liang was fortunate to have been raised by parents who did not follow Chinese tradition and have her feet bound. Her Father insisted his daughters become athletes and be well educated in academics, not just Chinese culture. She studied Chinese painting with her artist cousin who resided in the Emperor's Palace not far from where her family lived outside the Temple grounds. When her family immigrated to America, Pei Liang's sister became a well known tennis player and Pei Liang worked as a translator at the United Nations on 46th Street in Manhattan.

We met when I registered to take her painting class in Chinese landscape. Out of hundreds of students receiving instruction at the large university, somehow Pei Liang and I connected. We became close friends visiting each other's homes for more than 25 years until she developed Alzheimer's disease and could no longer recognize me as her friend.

In addition to painting, I learned a great deal about Chinese culture. Pei Liang once whispered to me, "In another life, you must have been Chinese, Ida."

She was referring to the paintings I had just completed in her Chinese Landscape class. As a first attempt, the completed pictures were good enough to frame and hang, which both surprised and pleased her at the time, and shocked me completely. I doubted I could ever paint anything as lovely as the Chinese watercolors I had seen in books and Museums. I thought about what she said to me and recalled I had always been fascinated with Chinese Classical Art.

Beginning at age eight, I remembered my fascination with painting Chinese ladies holding parasols, sitting or standing under cherry blossom trees. There was no particular reason why I chose to paint Asian scenes and people. My family was highly diversified with Europeans from Russia, Italy, Poland and Israel. Understanding the difference in their backgrounds was confusing enough for a very young child living in that diverse household. Why I became fascinated with the Chinese culture could be explained if one believed that in another life I had been born Chinese. At least that's what my friend Pei Liang gave as the reason for my ability to paint well in Chinese style. I accept that idea not necessarily believing it.

During the long hours as an Administrator for disenfranchised teenage youth I worked hard. I had always preferred the Artist's life, yet necessity forced me to relegate my passion to second place so that my two children and I could continue to eat.

While painting "Blue Mountains", I learned the importance of black ink, the Chinese love of the color "blue" and mastery of subject matter. In their work, the Chinese artist reflects an inner peace achieved through meditation before starting to paint. By rhythmic reworking brush strokes of bamboo over and over on newspaper, which was thrown out later, I managed to achieve the same mental therapeutic calm necessary to Chinese painting.

Perspective, used in Western or Renaissance Art does not exist in Chinese painting. The Chinese use placement of subjects on the rice paper to create the illusion of distance or importance as well as using distinctive brushstrokes to promote concepts.

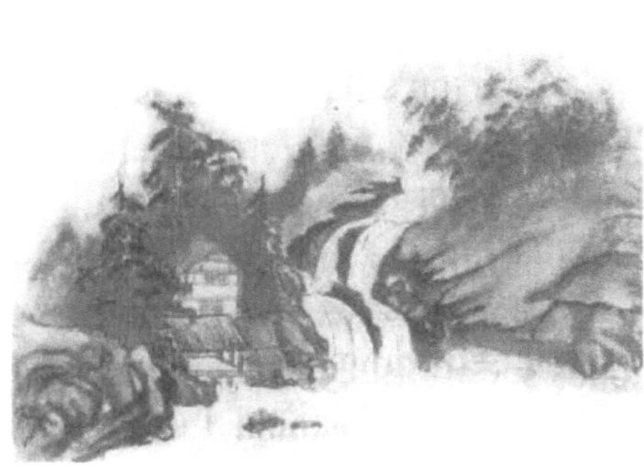 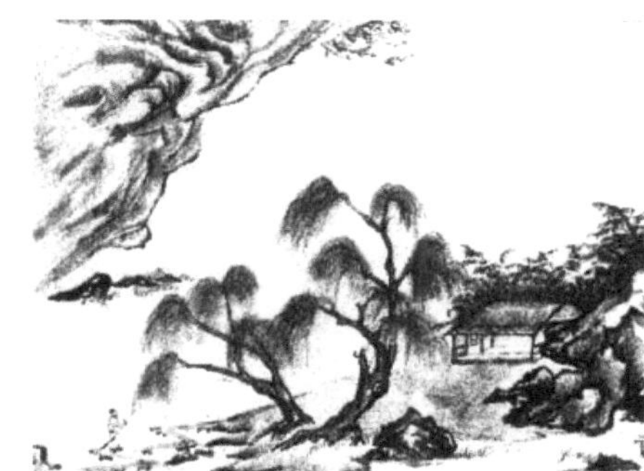

Personal status is suggested by painting someone larger in comparison to other persons or objects in the composition's scene. All detail is abstracted and held to a minimum. A lush forest is suggested with a few trees grouped with fewer leaves, with fewer branches and subdued color. Rivers or waterfalls resemble a strip of flowing ribbon suggesting life's blood as fundamental to universal energy. Rocks breathe and grasp the earth as if connected by giant animal paws. Clouds spew mist and their grayish flimsy powder-puff tones encircle mountains mysteriously.

To the Chinese mind, there are no empty spaces, only pieces of undisclosed knowledge. Behind every cloud, airplane, bird, or spirit ideas exist but are unseen. To the Chinese artist, there is always a message present everywhere.

For good quality, all brush strokes by the artist must be spontaneous and represent appropriate energy for the subject matter. The docile rabbit will not have the look of the lion, or the hair of the tiger. A Chinese painting's worth is determined by the emotion its completed version evokes.

The focus in Chinese painting is to abstract the "essence" of the subject, be it figure or object. Herein lays its appeal for me. I learned to visualize as an Asian artist would. Today, I can look at a landscape and see it simply in fewer lines, grey tones, and brush strokes without the need to be representational. As in their pictographic calligraphy, the Chinese approach to painting is animus, and is key to being recognized as different from western painting.

I may have met Pei Liang in the coldness of a New York winter but knowing her, brought many years of sunshine and happiness into my life.

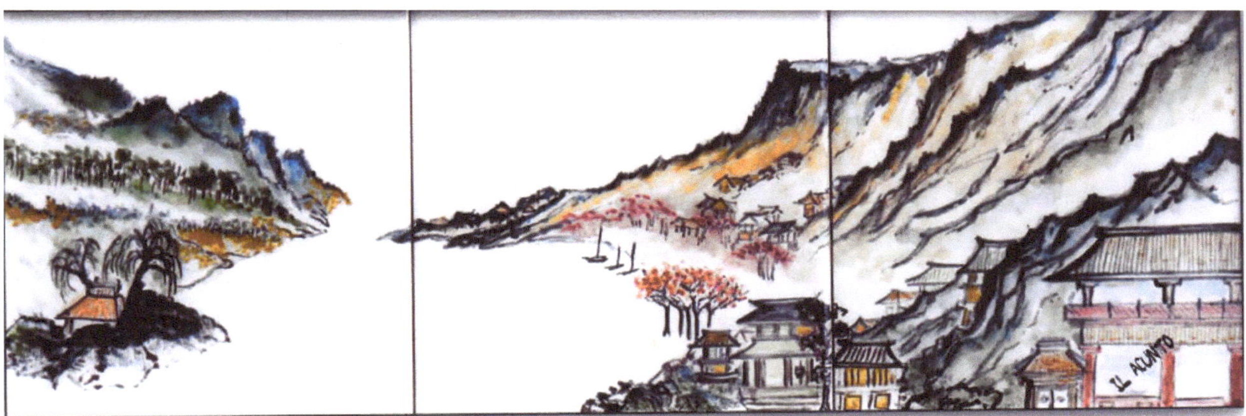

"MOUNTAIN TOWN"

Chinese paint on ceramic

Life's journey may be rocky or smooth

Either way you walk it alone!

"TALL PINES @ RIVERS EDGE"

Chinese landscape / rice paper / framed under glass

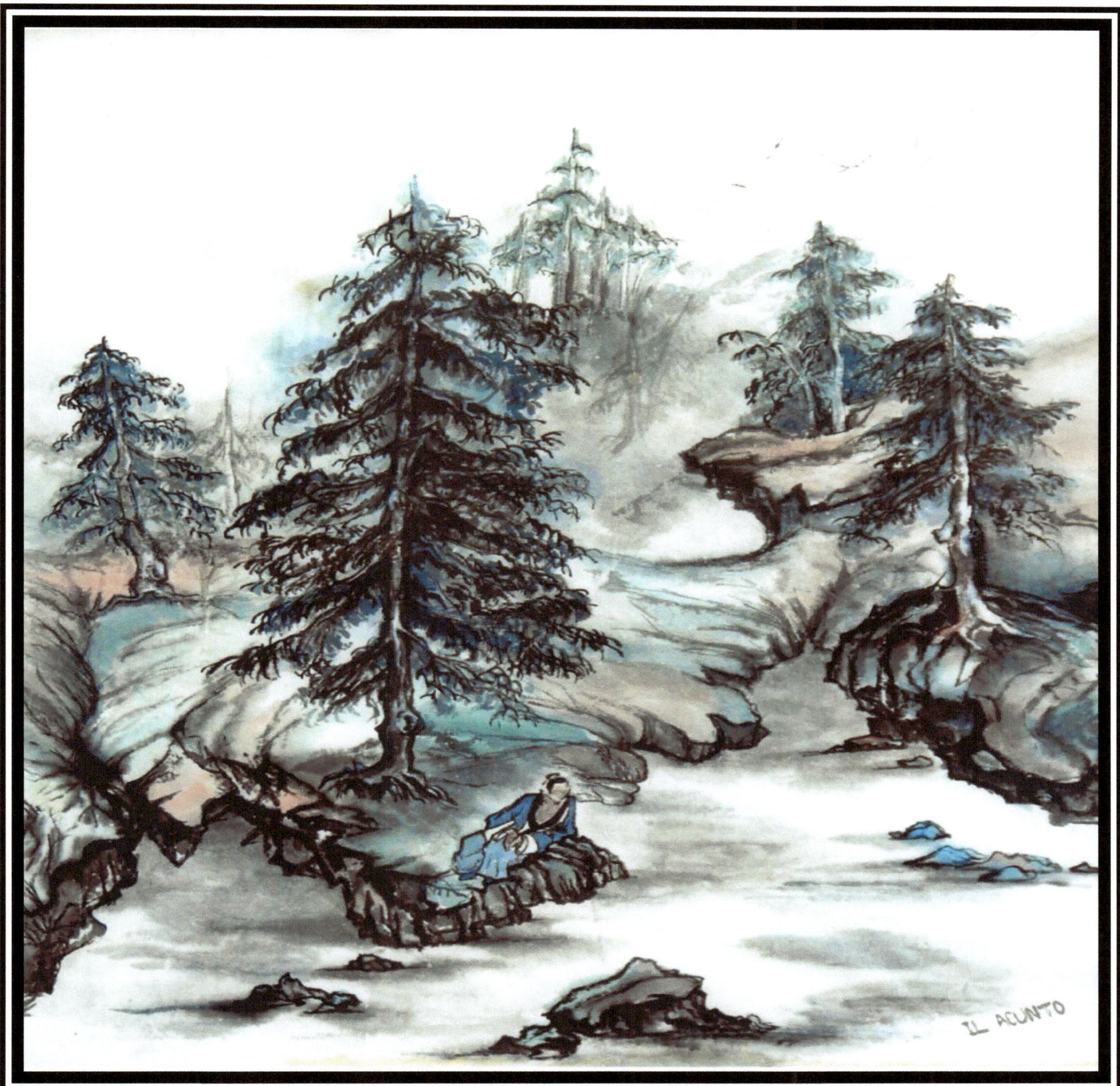
IL ACUNTO

The hearth of a home is in the soul

Of those who live within

"TREE HOUSE"

Chinese watercolor on rice paper (16"W x 28"H) framed

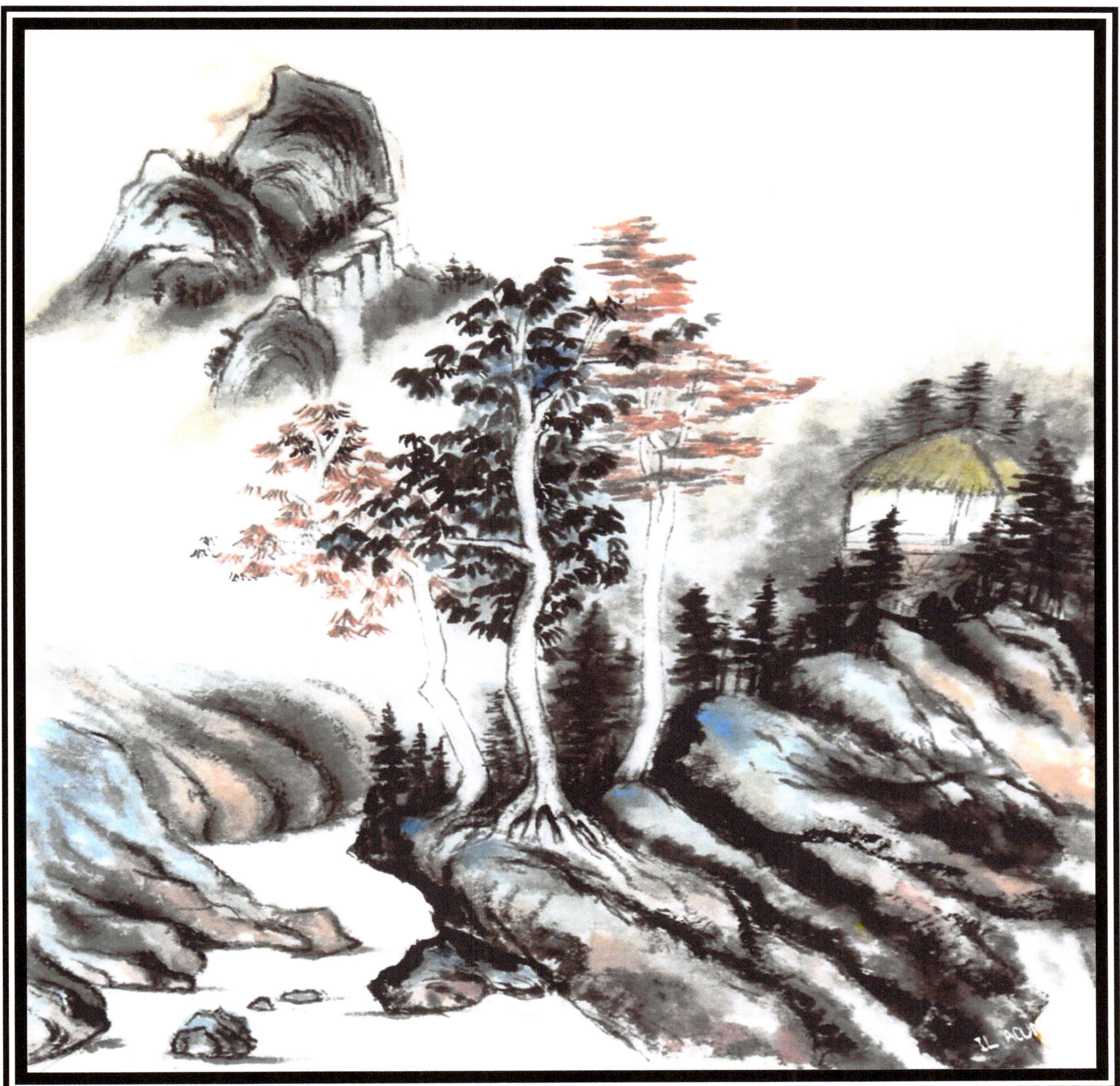

A cloudless world reaps no harvest

Water color on rice paper (16"W x 28"H) framed under glass

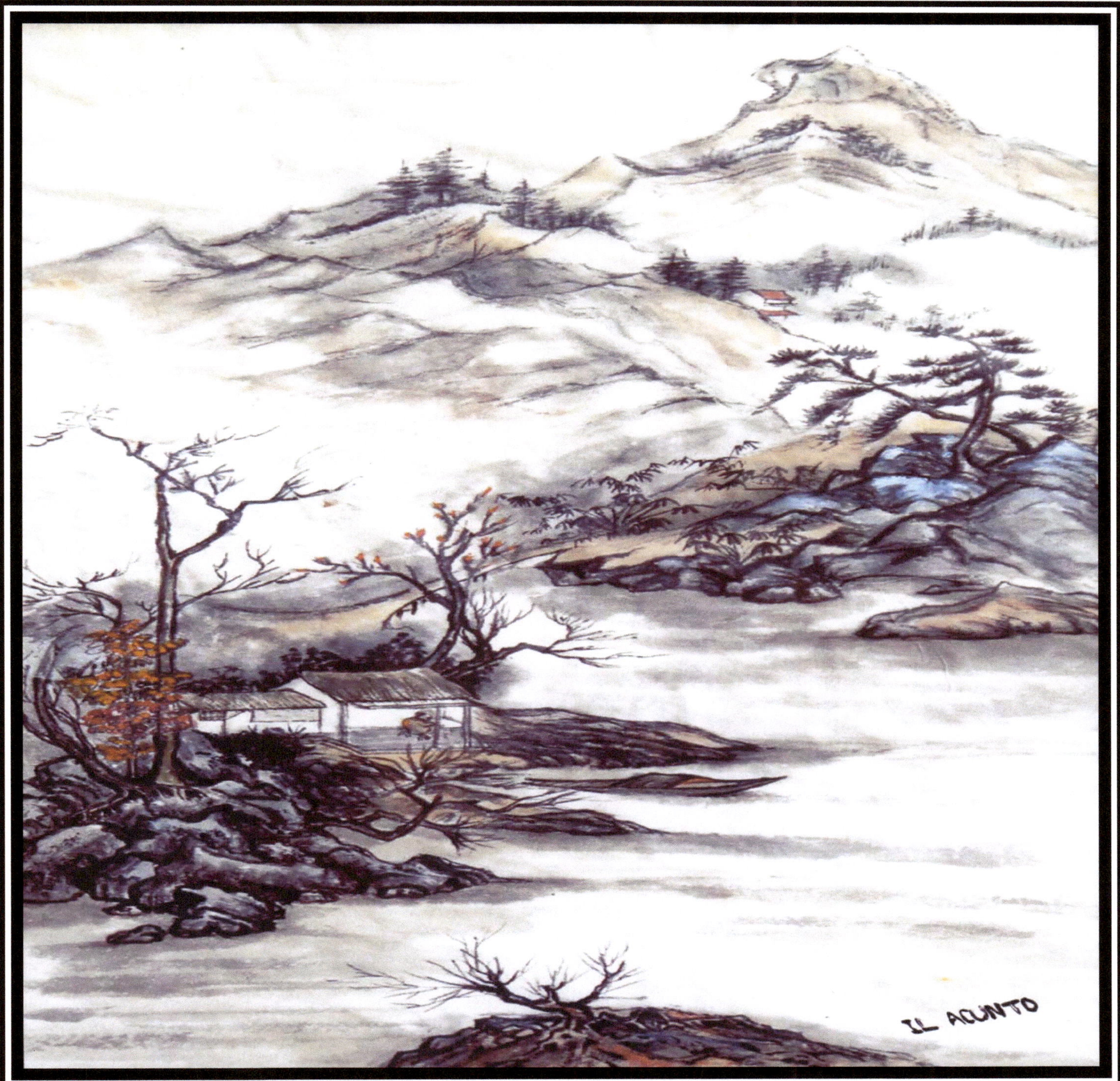
IL ACUNTO

Life is cruel in its brevity
Our moments are too wonderful
To realize and hold.

"HOUSE AT ROCK MOUNTAIN"

Chinese landscape / rice paper / framed under glass

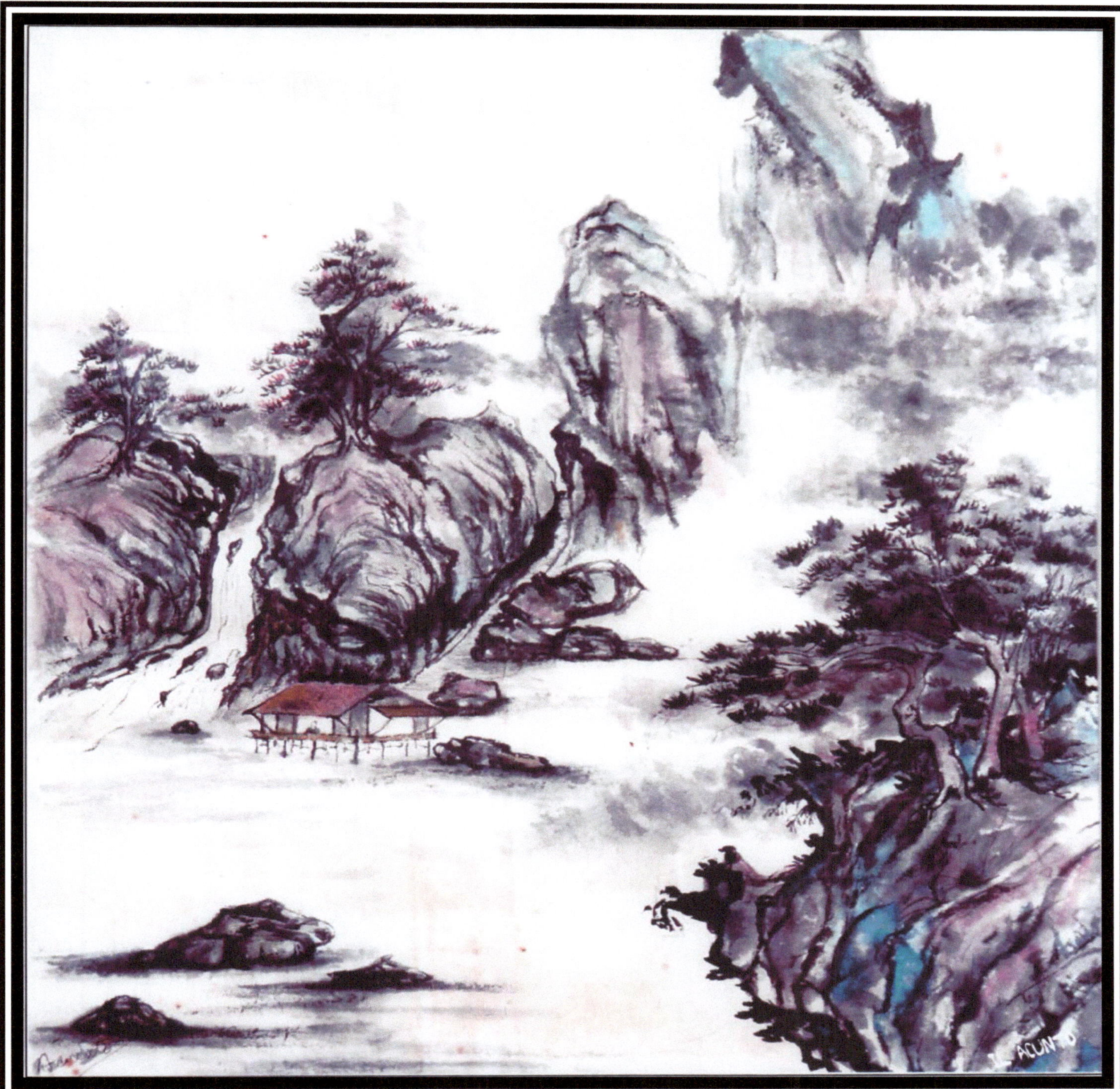

The true scholar seeks learning

without end

Chinese landscape on rice paper (17"W x 20"H) framed

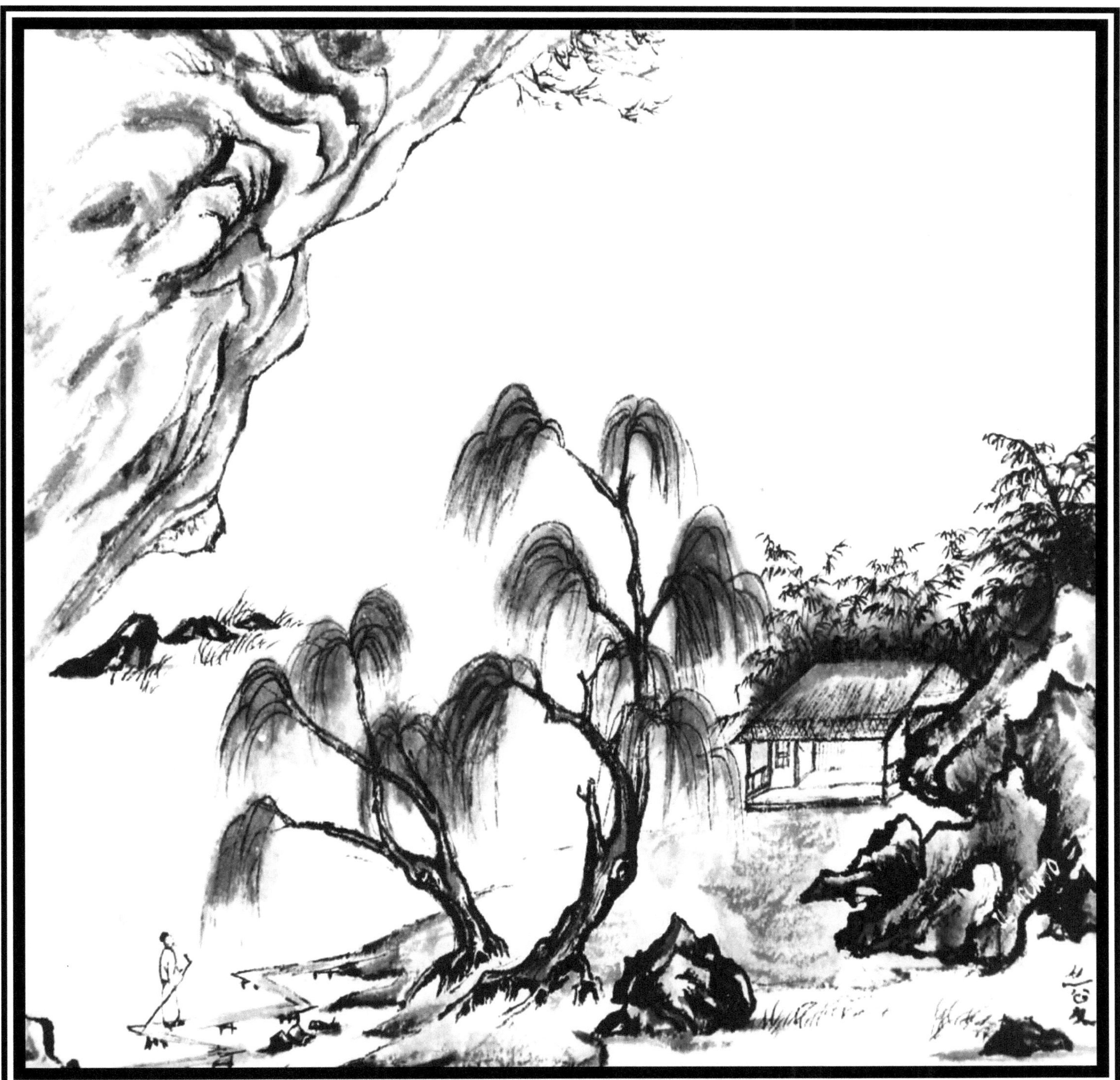

Give me the simple folk
When they abuse you
At least you know why.

"WOMAN ON BRIDGE"

Paint on ceramic plate in wood frame

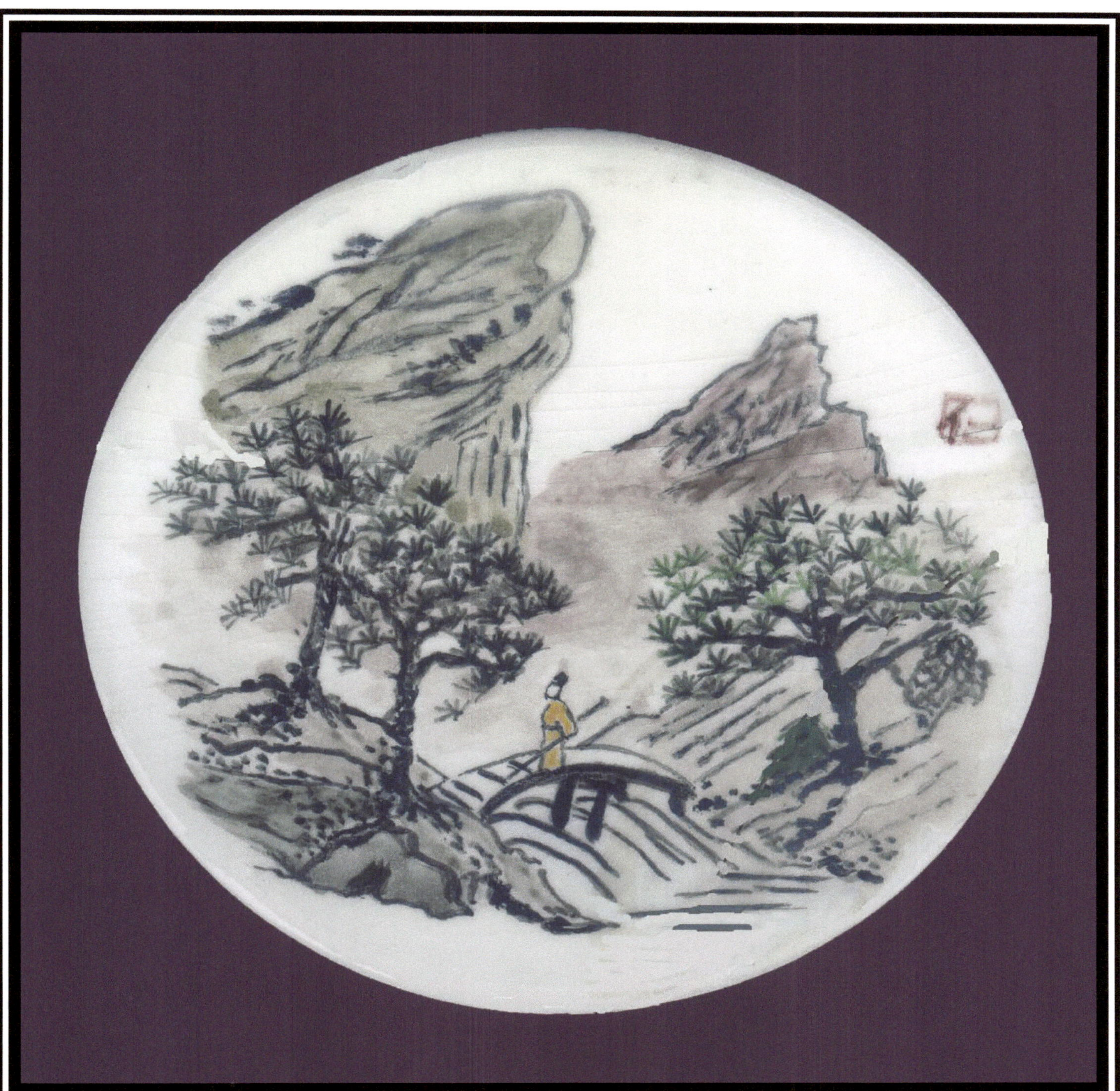

A rose without thorns

Loses its scent

"FLOWER WITH FISH"

Chinese style watercolor on rice paper (8"W x 22"H)

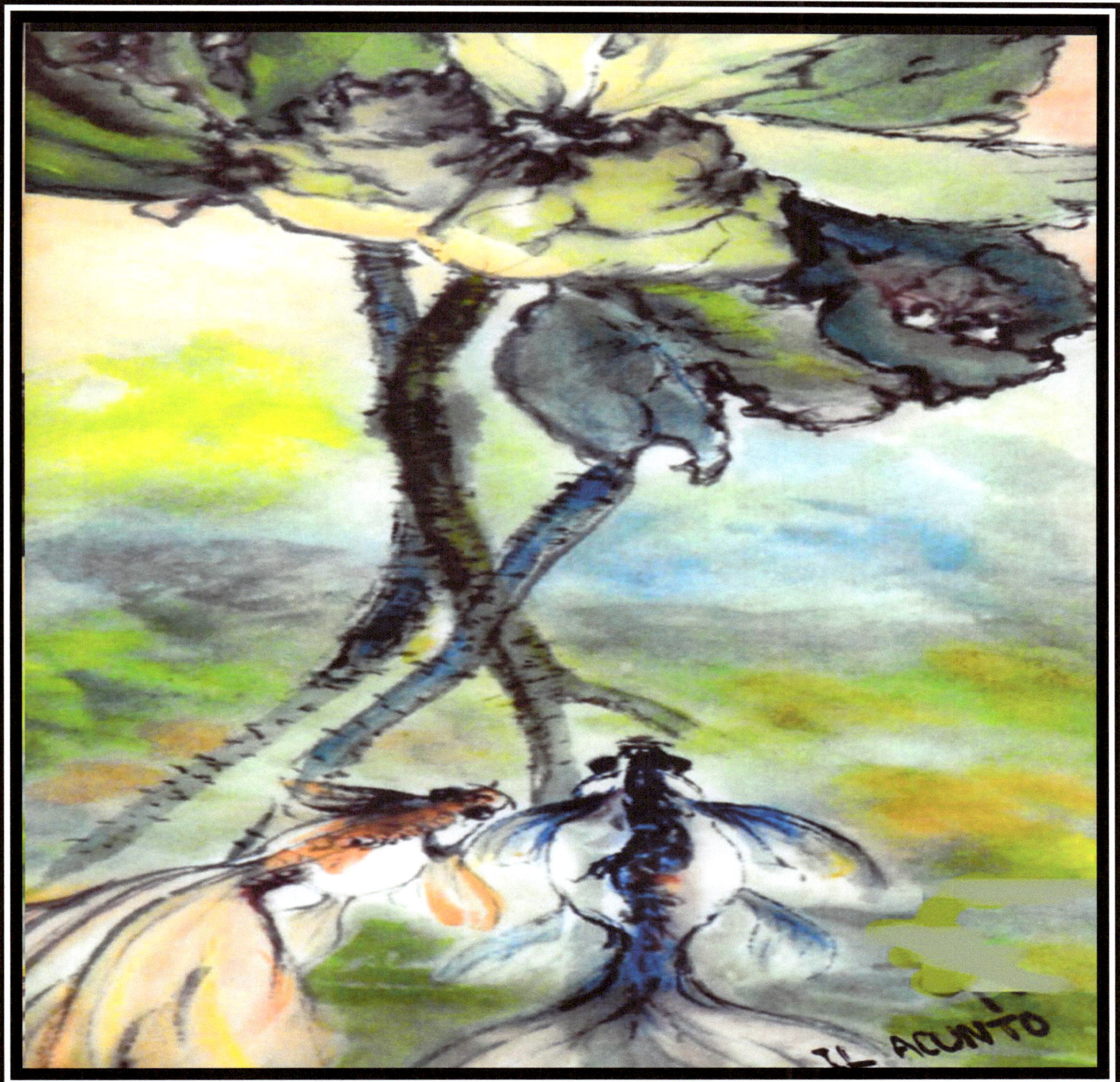

ACUNTO

Transcending the ordinary

Marks a lonely road.

"LADY ON BIRCH TREE"

Watercolor on silk

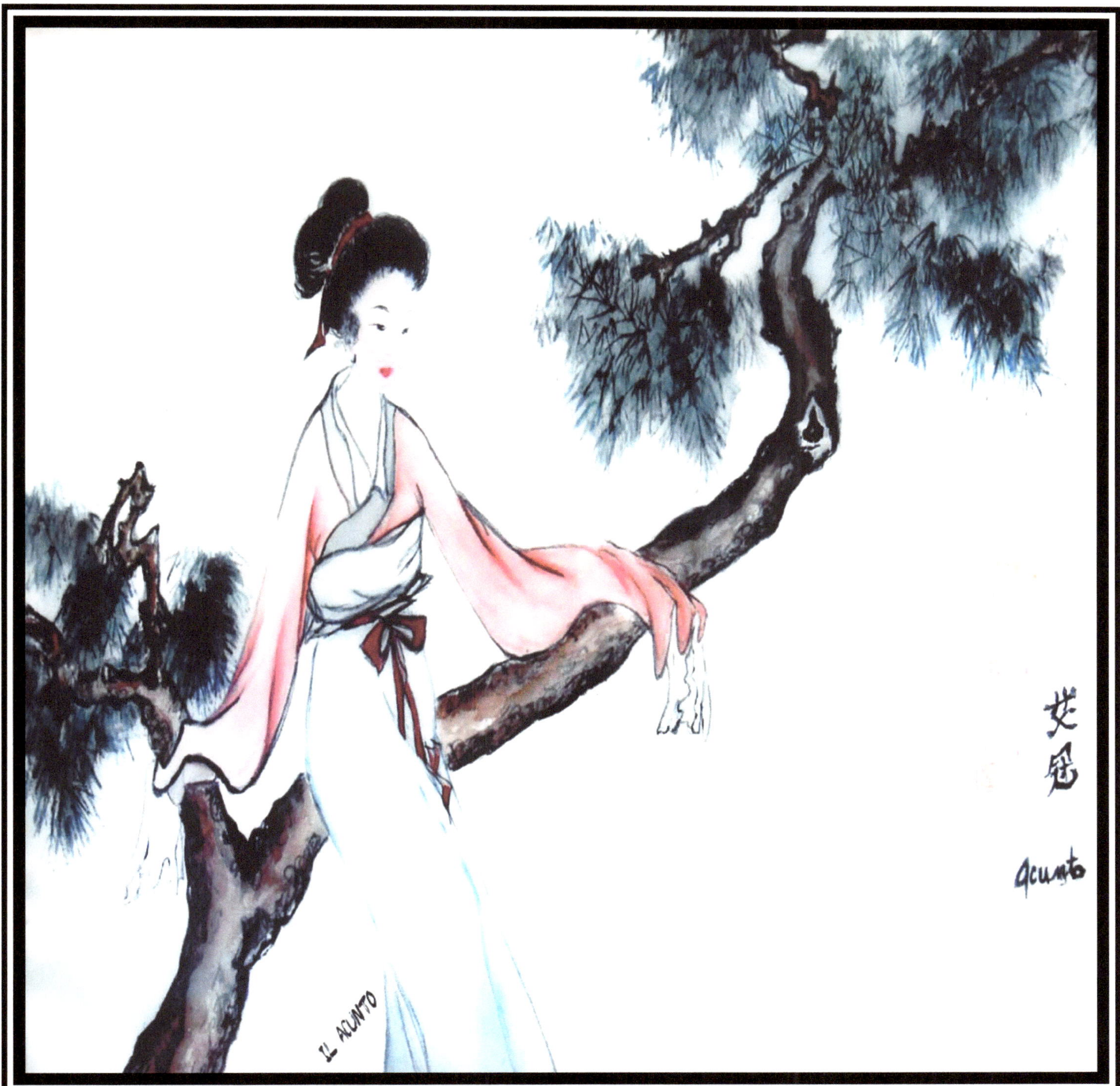

Beyond the misty clouds
is the clearing
Catch its memory
before it's blown away

"THE CLEARING"

Chinese watercolor on rice paper framed under glass

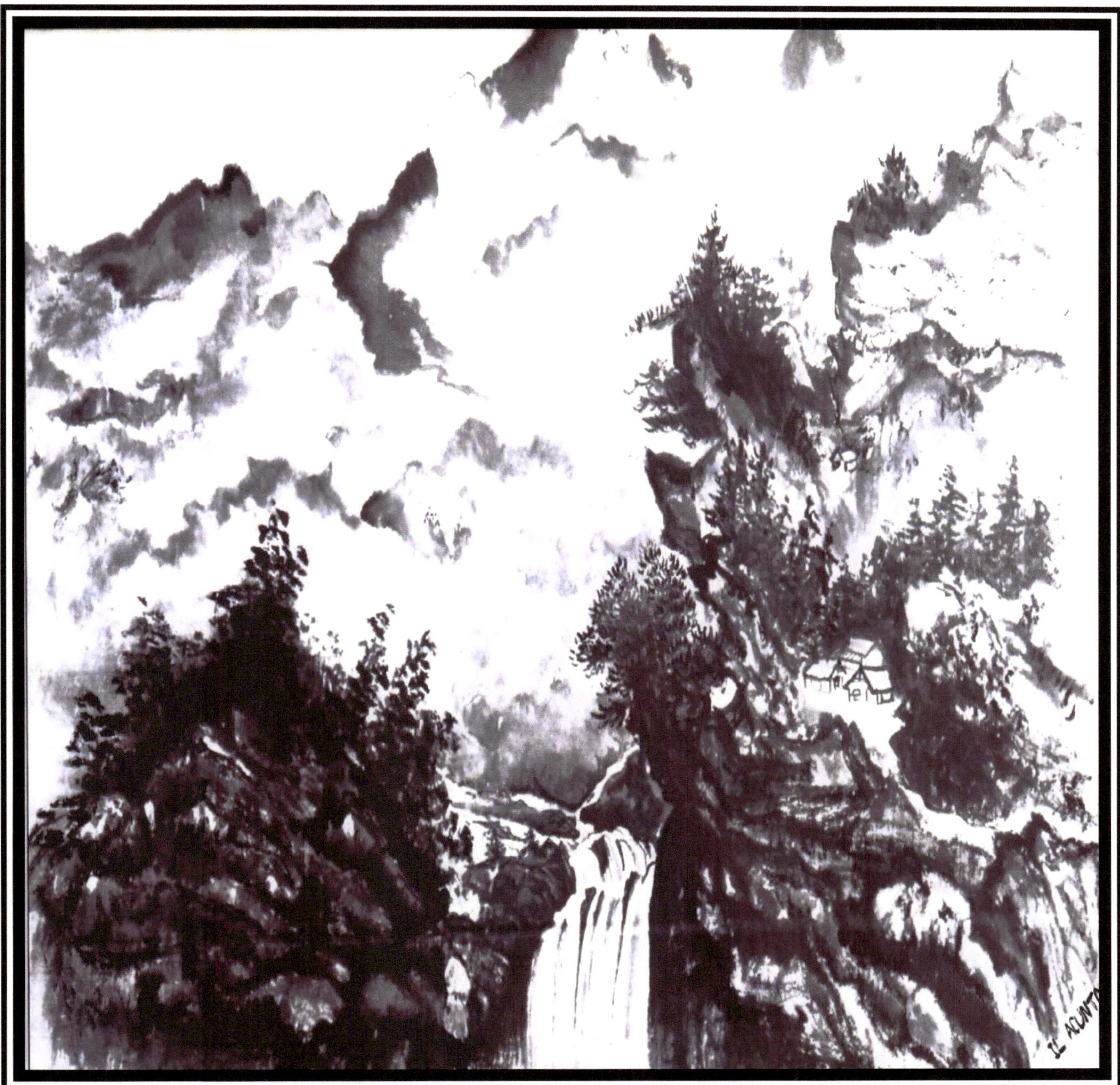

Gathering seeds in the wind
brings hope for new beginnings

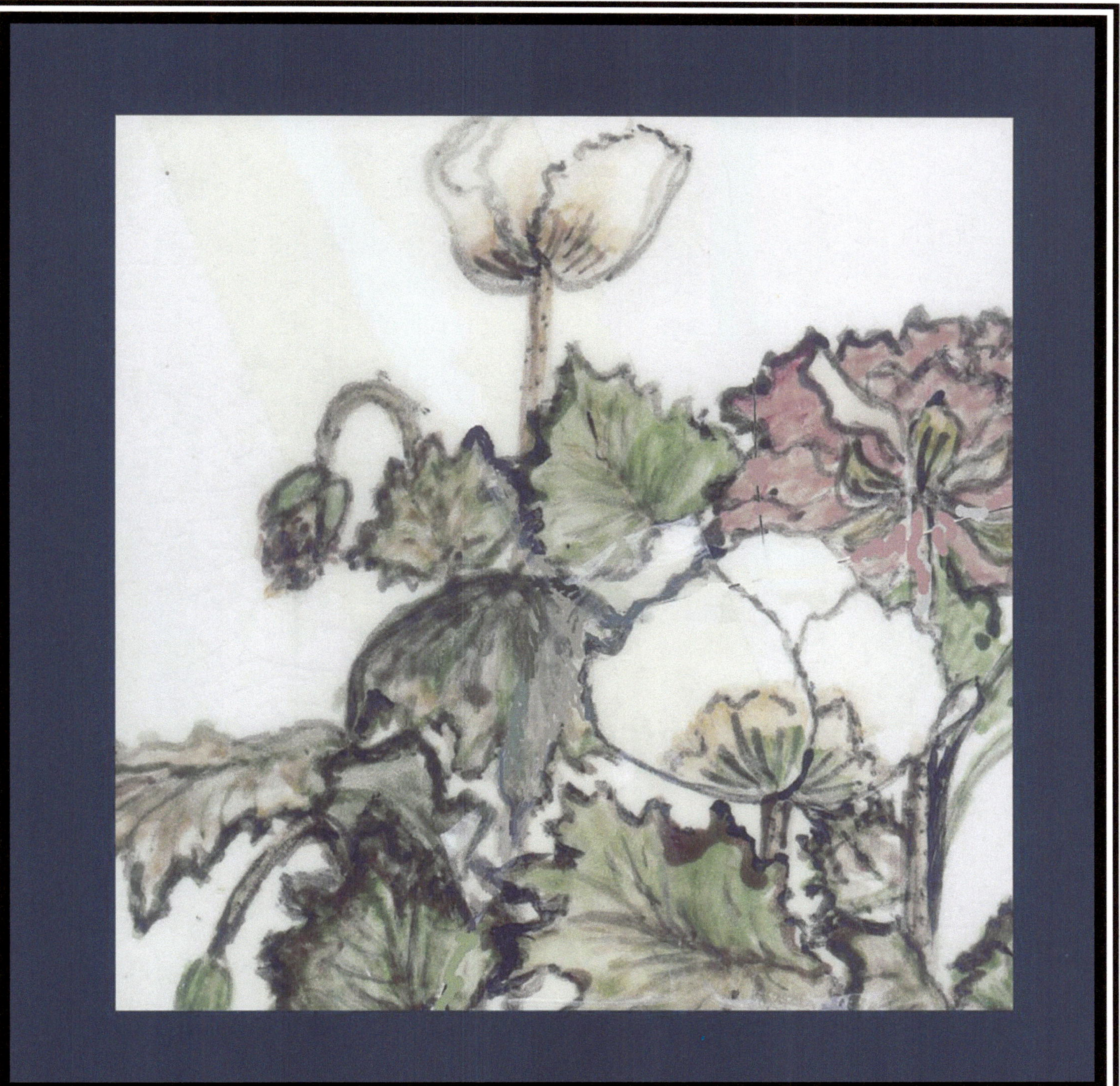

The Other Side

Catch a walk to the other side,
There is the mountain...
Walk mid raindrops of torrential
Power...
Grab on to passing clouds across the tops
Go gently...
Do not disturb the Eagle's nest.

"SCENE IN ROCKS"

Chinese tea silk screen.

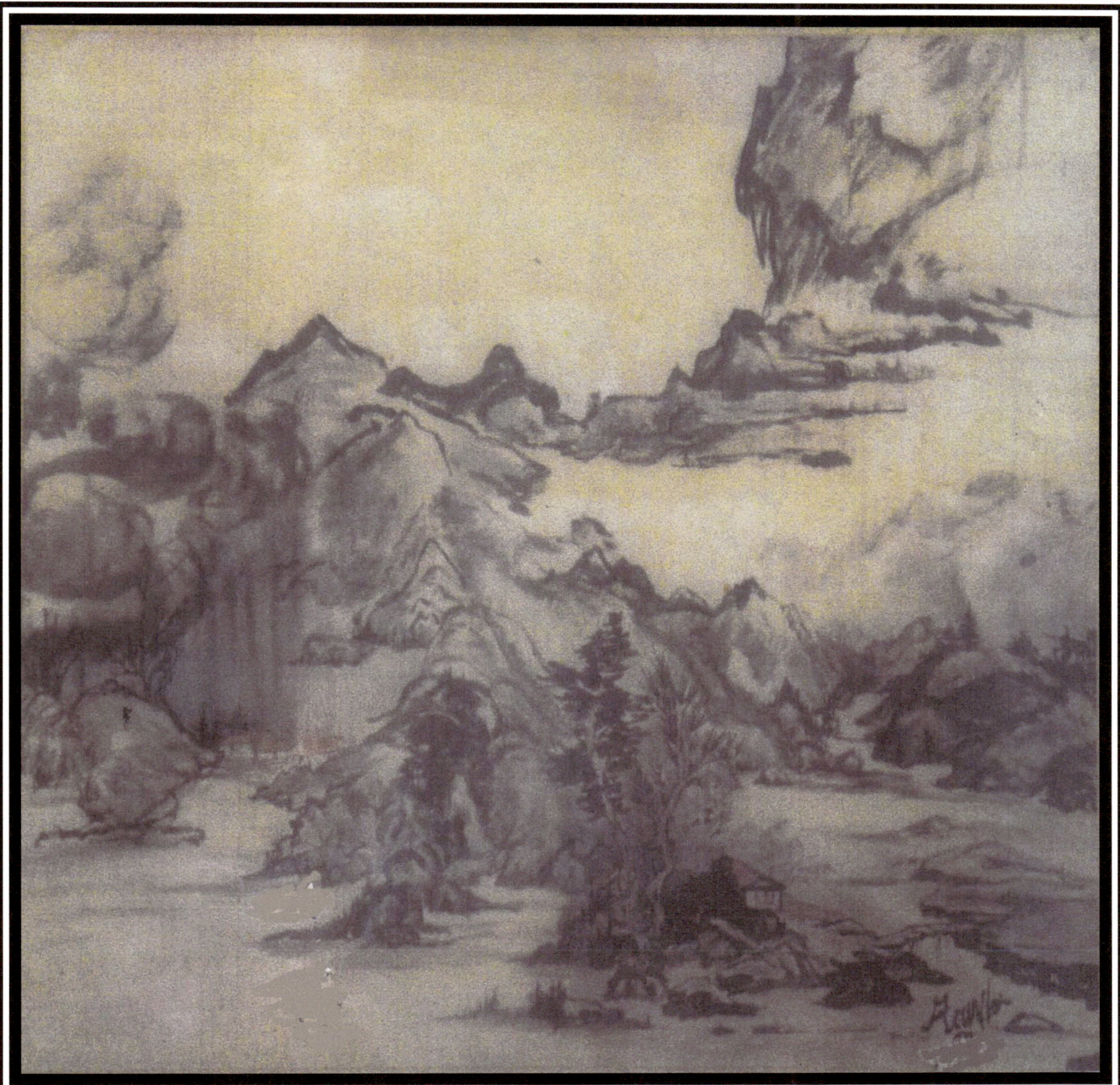

Bamboo shoots bending easily
Never lose their ground.

"WATER STREAM BY BAMBOO"

Chinese landscape / rice paper (31"W x 18")

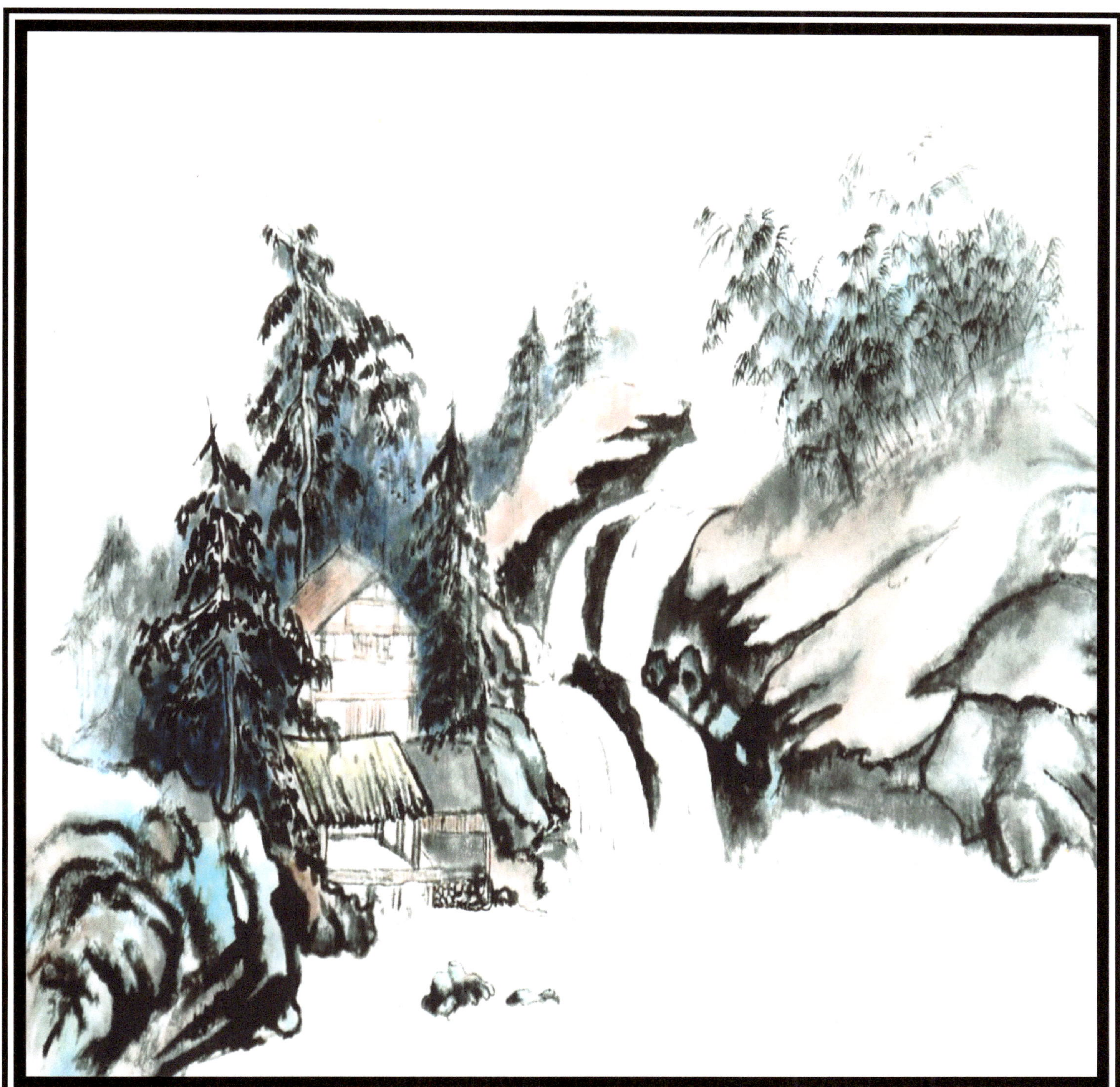

Without loyalty no village is born.

"THE VALLEY"

Chinese landscape / watercolors.

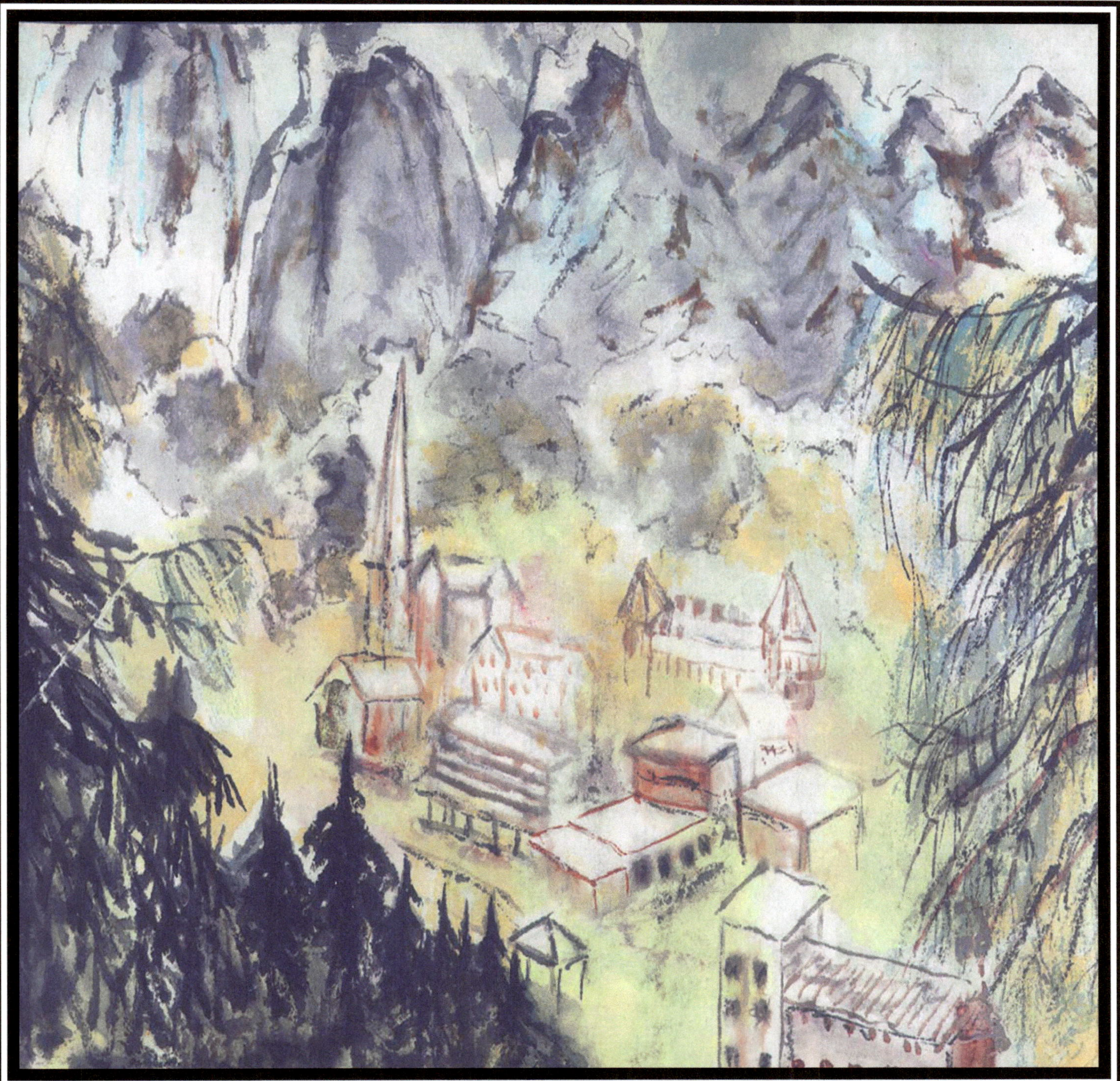

All life is choice,

Blame no one for the outcome.

"WATER LILLY"

Chinese watercolor on parchment.

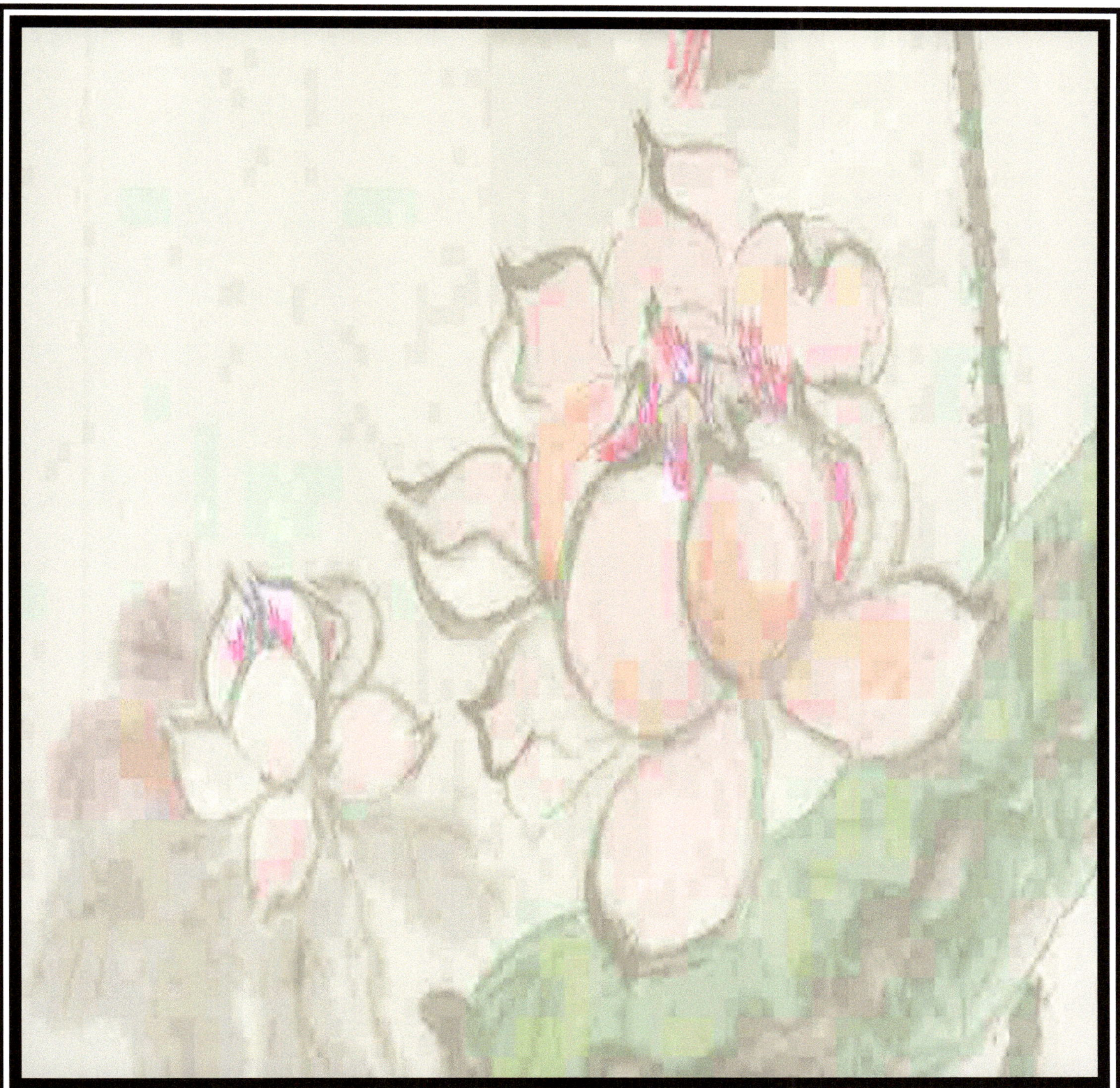

From the earth grew the spirit that
Guides the river of our soul.

"MAN IN BATEAU"

Chinese watercolor on rice paper

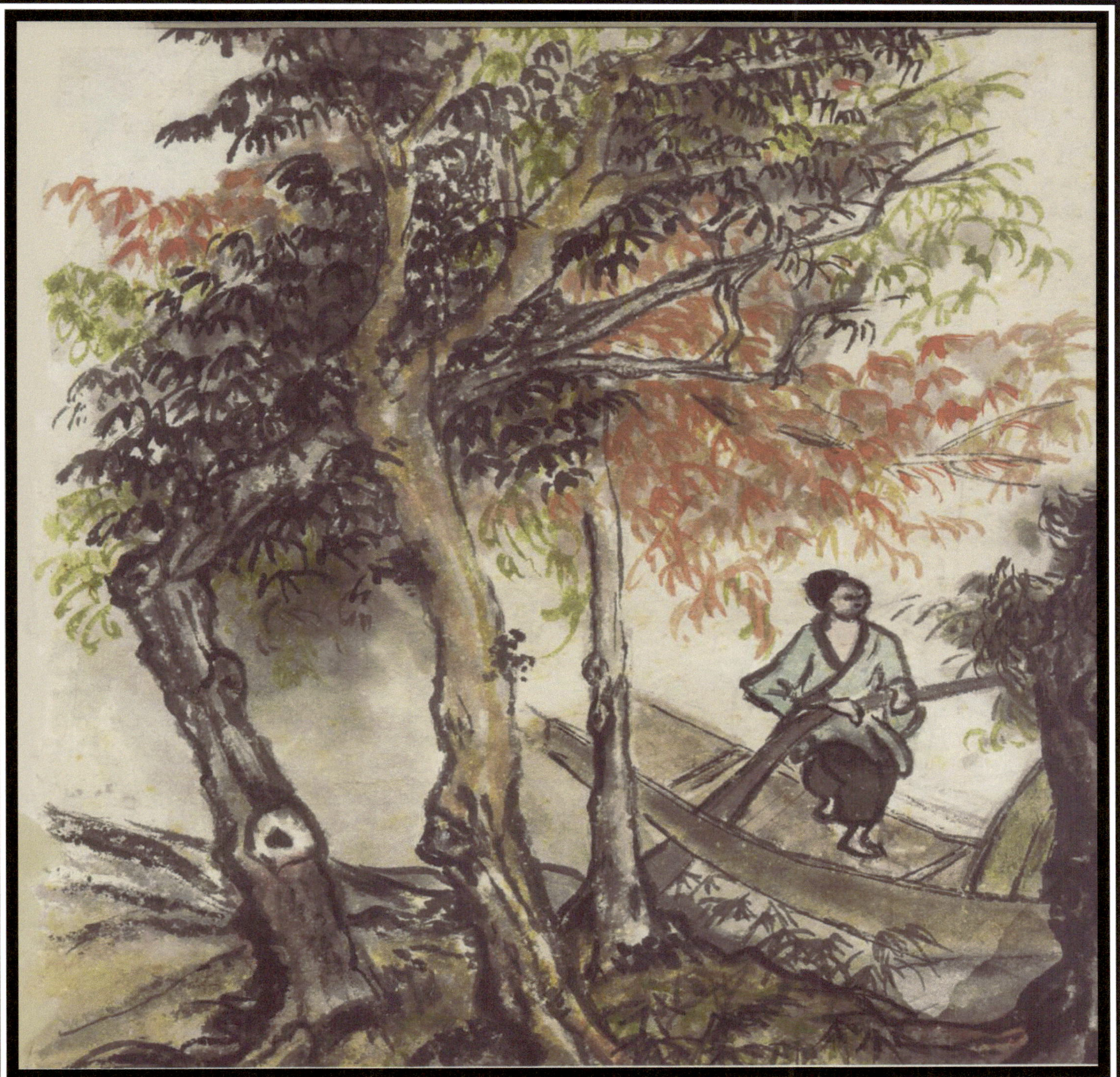

On Youth's Passage

How sweet the Berry on the Vine,

Dull flushed Bright Red to intertwine

With one's view of Man's ungracious Nature.

How long will Berries sit so ripe,

To tease one's sight and blind with pleasure?

Such Beauty is not forever,

Drink in its lusciousness while it lasts!

"BERRIES ON THE VINE"

Chinese ink on rice paper

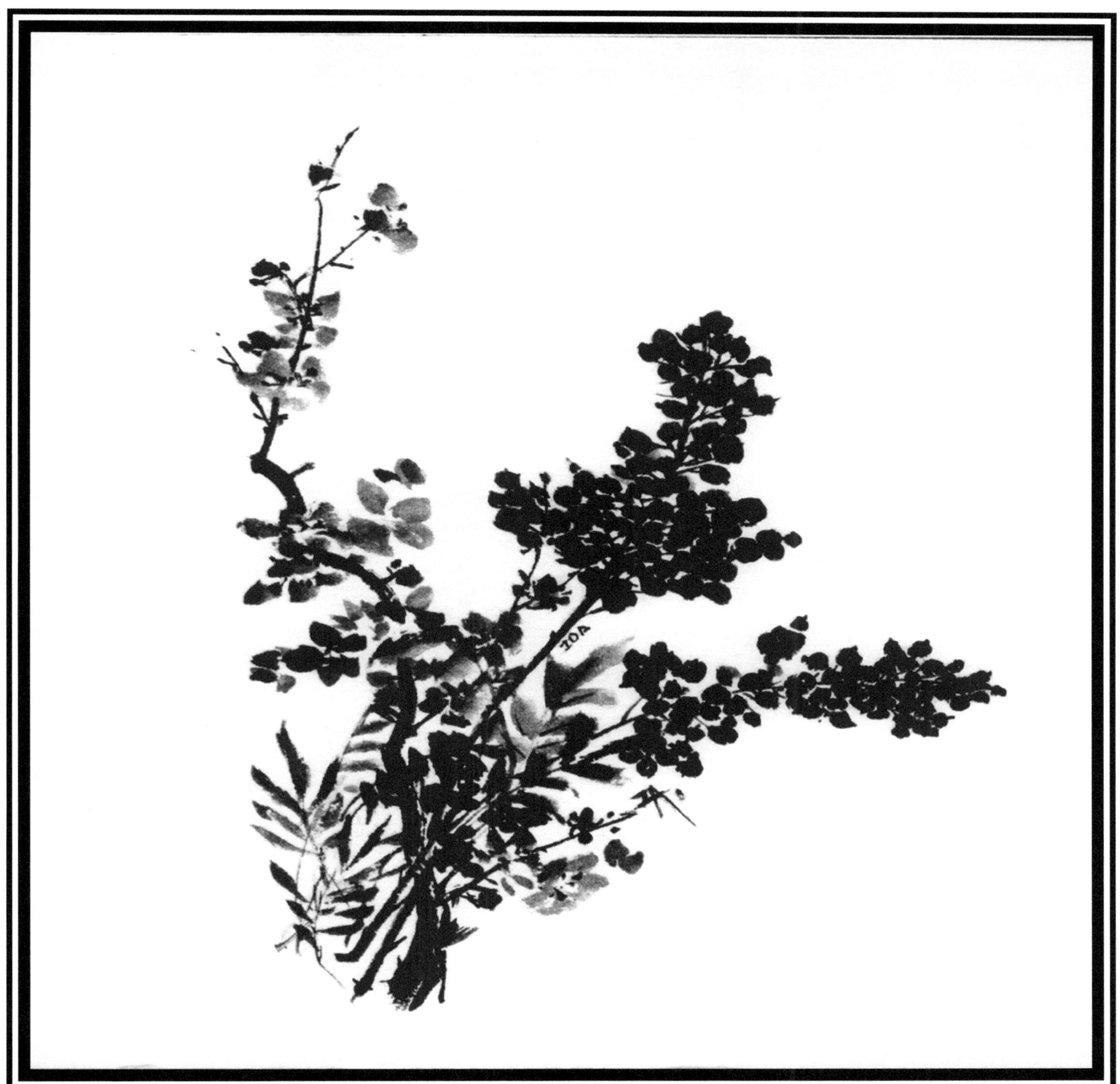

Twisted Pines

Branches rooted together
Held too hard
In opposite directions
Twist off to die alone

"TWISTED PINE"

Chinese ink and watercolor on rice paper

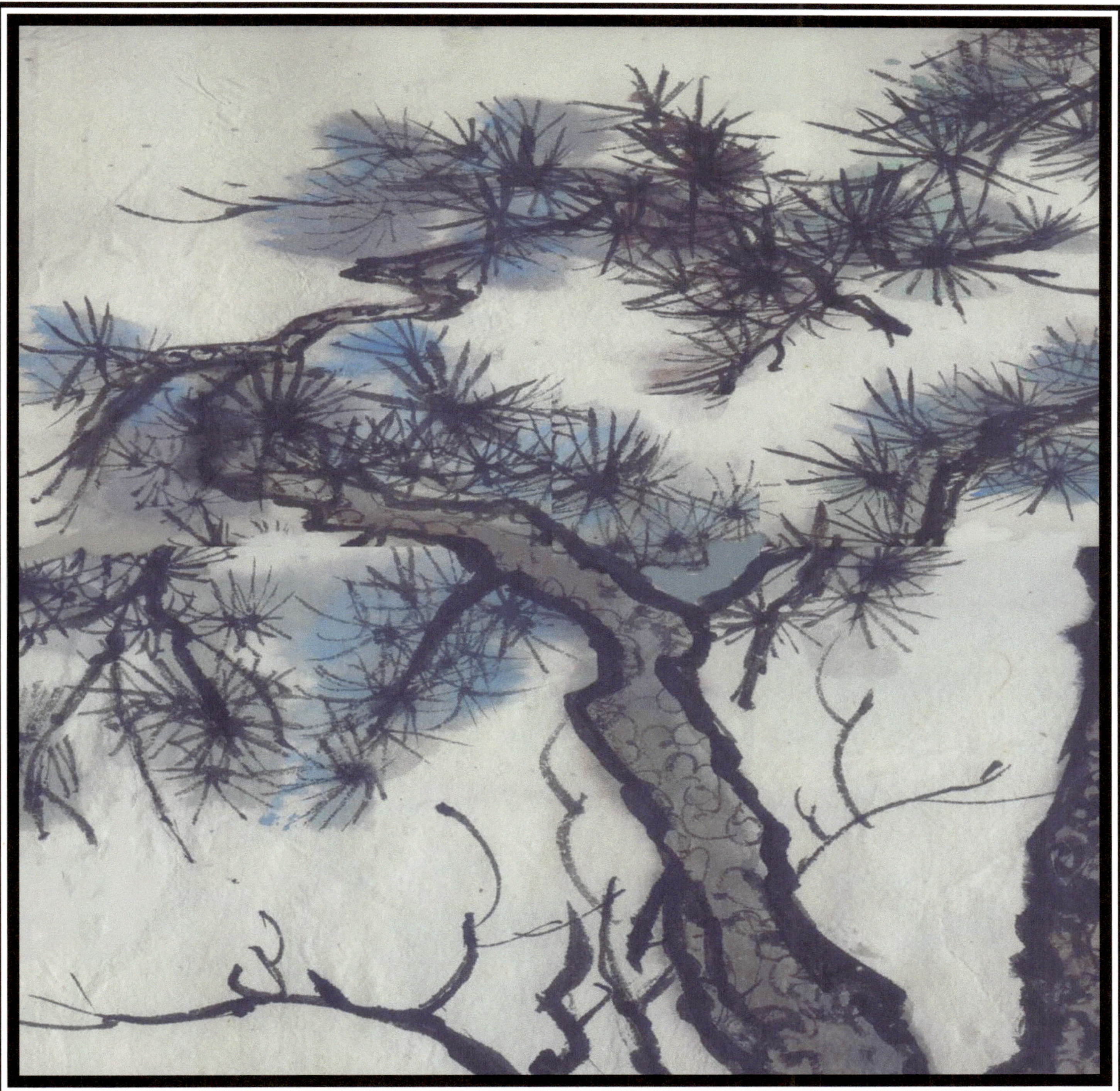

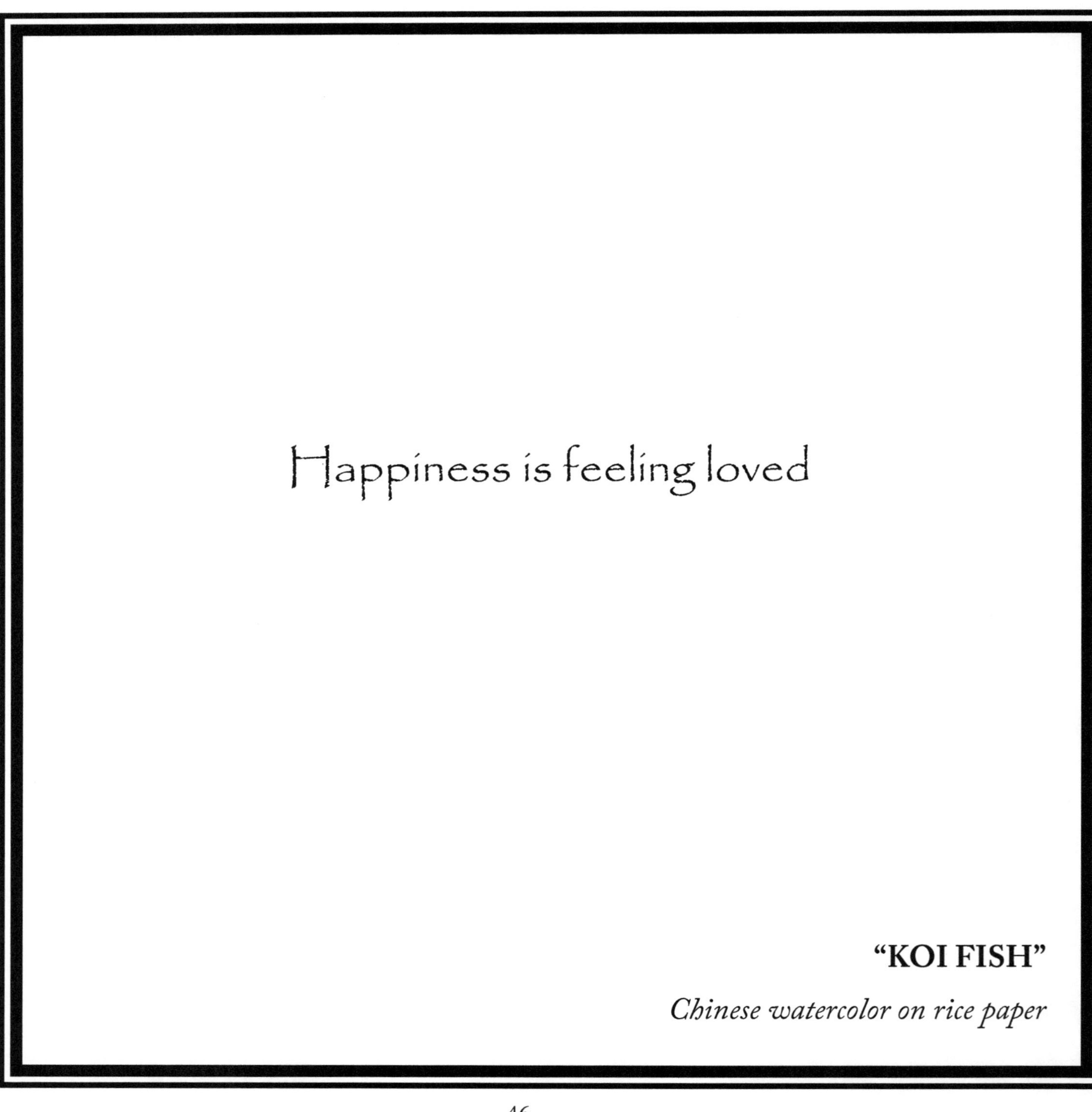

Happiness is feeling loved

"KOI FISH"

Chinese watercolor on rice paper

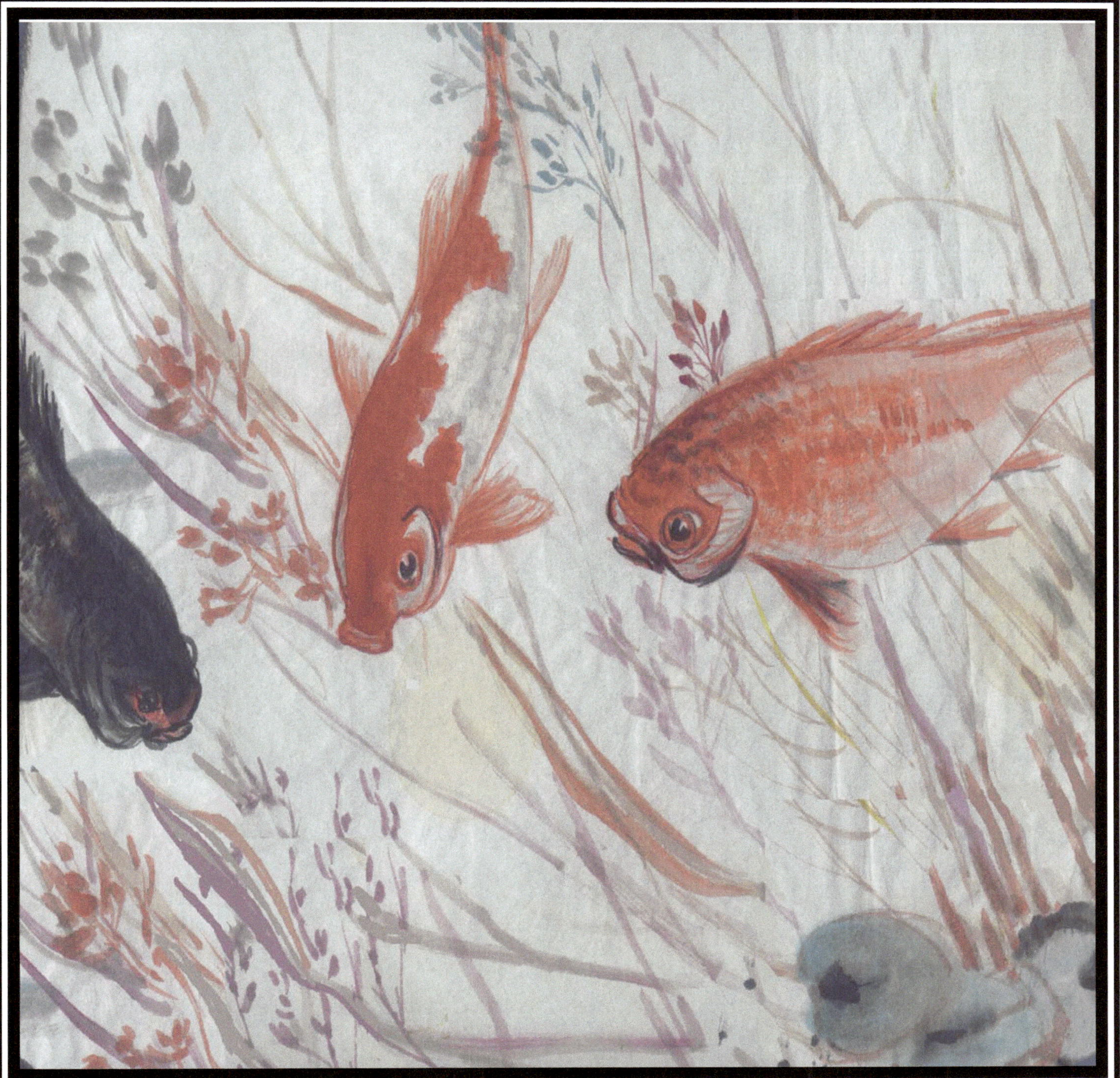

Winter's night refuels the spirit

with summer's heat

"HOUSE IN THE WOODS"

Chinese watercolor on rice paper

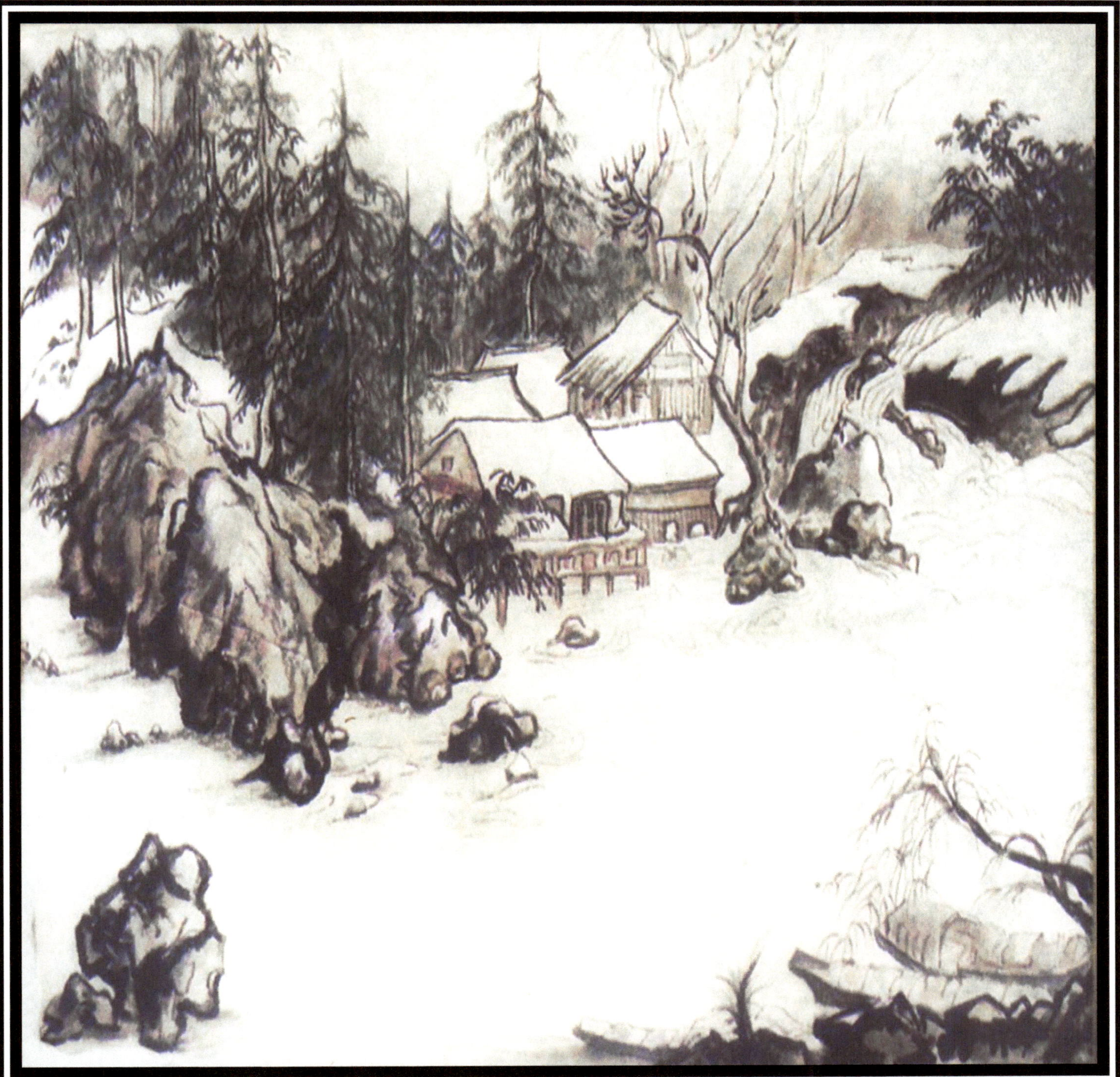

Keeping to the high road
Guarantees safe arrival

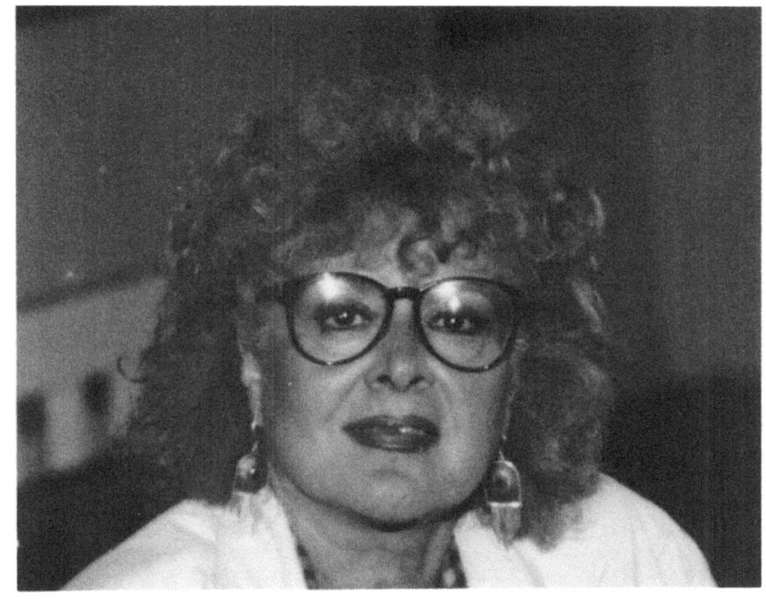

Ida Lillian Acunto
Author/Artist/Educator

Mary Ann Peck, Editor

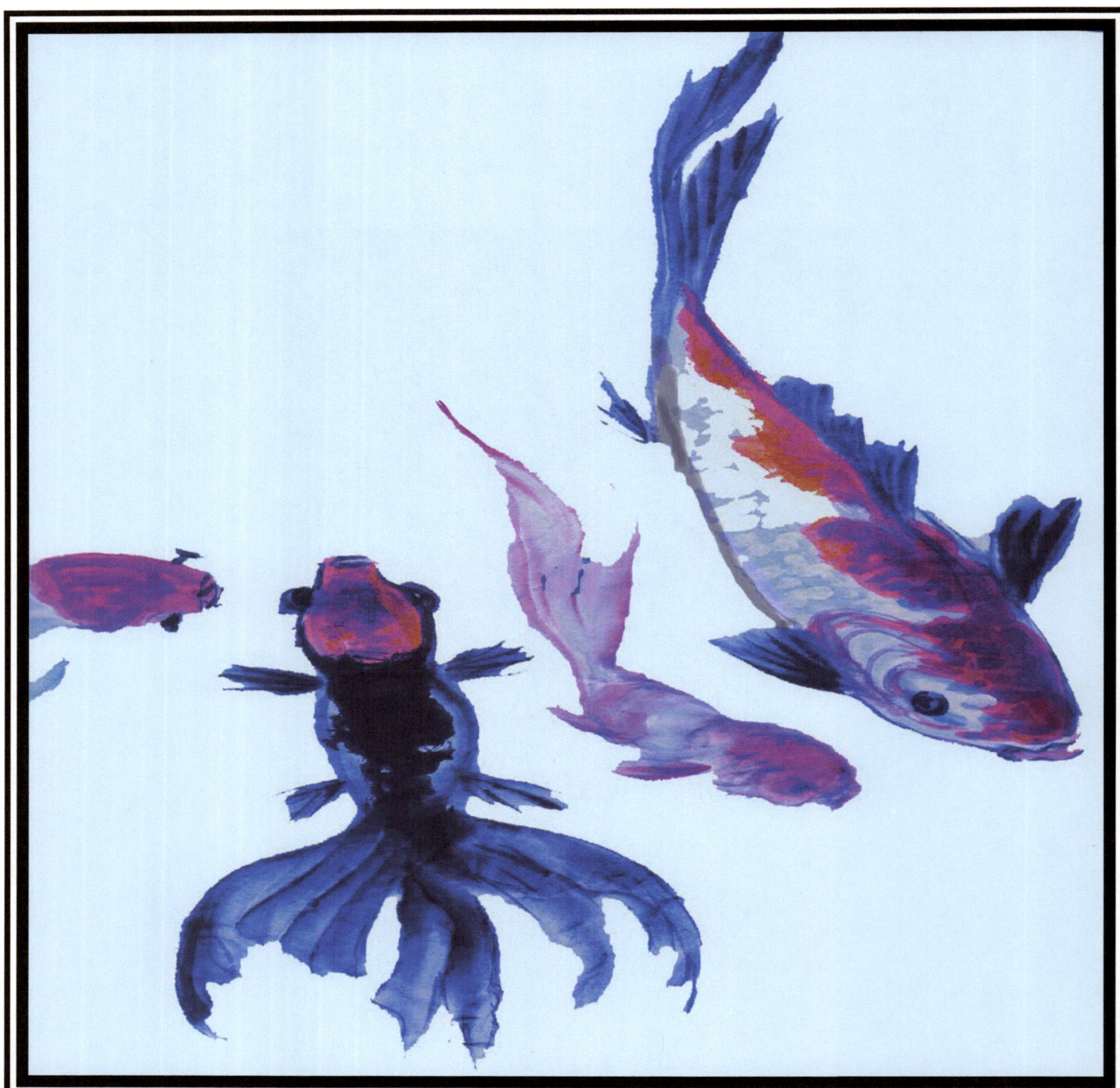